Armenia travel guide
2023 - 2024

Armenia: The Modern Face of a
Timeless Nation

Daniel B. Sharer

Table of content

Chapter 1: Introduction to Armenia

Armenia, a land of old history and stunning scenery, is a secret gem tucked in the South Caucasus area of Eurasia. This chapter will provide you with an informed review of Armenia's geography, location, cultural history, and important travel tips to ensure a memorable and enjoyable trip.

Armenia's Geography and Location:

Armenia is an isolated country in the South Caucasus, surrounded by Turkey to the west, Georgia to the north, Azerbaijan to the east, and Iran to the south. Despite its relatively small size, Armenia is a land of different and differing scenery. The country's scenery runs from lush valleys and rolling hills to rocky mountains, which make up a large part of the landscape.

One of the most famous natural features of Armenia is Mount Ararat, a beautiful extinct volcano that is historically important as the traditional resting place of Noah's Ark. Although Mount Ararat is located just across the border in Turkey, its tall presence is visible from many parts of Armenia, acting as a sign of national identity and pride.

The beautiful Lake Sevan, often referred to as the "jewel of Armenia," is another notable natural feature. This high-altitude lake, one of the biggest in the world, provides a beautiful contrast to the nearby mountains and offers chances for water-based sports and rest.

Brief History and Cultural Heritage:

Armenia's past is rooted in antiquity, with proof of human villages going back thousands of years. It is known as one of the oldest Christian nations, publicly accepting Christianity as the state faith in 301 AD, long before many other countries in the world.

Throughout its past, Armenia has experienced times of freedom and wealth, as well as foreign attacks and control. Various powers, including the Roman, Byzantine, Persian, and Ottoman, have ruled over Armenia, leaving behind a mix of cultural effects.

The Armenian people have experienced numerous challenges, including the Armenian Genocide of 1915, which saw the mass killings and deportations of Armenians under the Ottoman Empire. Despite these challenges, the resiliency of the Armenian spirit remains obvious in their rich cultural history and customs.

The Armenian language, an Indo-European language with unique writing, plays a key role in keeping the nation's character and ties to its historical past. Armenian literature, music, and arts have thrived over the ages, with famous poets, musicians, and artists adding to the country's artistic history.

Essential Travel Tips and Safety Information:

Before starting on your journey to Armenia, it's essential to consider some basic travel tips to ensure an easy and enjoyable experience:

Entry Requirements and Visa Regulations: Ensure that you have a current passport with at least six months of validity from your trip dates. Depending on your country, you may need to apply for a visa before coming to Armenia.

Check the latest visa rules and needs from the nearest Armenian office or consulate.

Best Time to Visit Armenia: Armenia experiences four different seasons. Spring (April to June) and fall (September to November) are usually considered the best times to visit due to warmer weather and blooming landscapes. Summer (June to August) can be hot, especially in lower areas, while winters (December to February) can be quite cold, giving chances for snow sports fans.

Packing Essentials for Different Seasons: Pack properly for the season you'll be going in. In warmer months, bring lightweight clothes, comfy walking shoes, and sun protection. In colder months, pack warm clothes, a waterproof jacket, and strong boots for possible snow sports.

Currency and Money Matters: The official currency of Armenia is the Armenian Dram (AMD). ATMs are widely available in cities and towns, and credit cards are accepted at most hotels, restaurants, and bigger businesses. However, it's wise to take some cash, especially when visiting more rural places or local markets.

Armenia is usually a safe place for visitors, but like any area, it's important to stay alert and practice common sense. Respect local practices and traditions, and be careful of your things, especially in busy places.

With this information in hand, you're now ready to start on an amazing trip to explore the wonders of Armenia! Whether you're captivated by its old history, amazed by its natural beauty, or enchanted by its warm welcome, Armenia promises to leave an everlasting mark on your heart and soul.

Chapter 2: Getting Ready for Your Trip

As you embark on your journey to Armenia, careful preparation is crucial to ensure a smooth and enjoyable experience.

This chapter goes deeper into essential aspects of planning your trip, including visa requirements and entry rules, the best time to visit Armenia, packing items for different seasons, and important information about currency and money issues.

1. Visa Requirements and Entry Regulations:

Before you set off on your trip to Armenia, it's important to familiarize yourself with the country's visa standards and entry rules. The rules can change based on your country, the goal of your visit, and the length of your stay. Citizens of certain countries may be qualified for visa-free travel, while others may need to receive a visa in advance.

To discover the exact visa needs for your country, check the official website of the Armenian government or get in touch with the nearest Armenian office or consulate. Keep in mind that visa handling times may change, so it's wise to apply well in advance to avoid any last-minute difficulties.

2. Best Time to Visit Armenia:

Armenia's environment is different, giving unique views throughout the year. Each season has its charm, so picking the best time to visit relies on your interests and tastes.

Spring (April to June) is a lovely time to explore Armenia, as nature bursts into bloom, painting the scenery with bright colors. The weather is warm, making it ideal for sightseeing, climbing, and soaking yourself in the country's rich cultural history. The famous Yerevan Wine Days festival, held in May, is a must-attend event for wine lovers.

If you prefer better weather and enjoy outdoor activities, try coming during the summer months (June to August). The days are longer, giving more time to tour sites and join in fairs and events. Just be prepared for the higher temperatures, especially if you plan to visit areas with lower levels.

Autumn (September to October) is another great time to visit Armenia. The weather stays nice, and the fields are adorned with the beautiful colors of fall. The Armenian Highland Festival, featuring traditional music, dance, and crafts, is a highlight during this season.

For winter fans and sports enthusiasts, the winter months (December to February) offer a unique experience. Snow-covered scenery and the chance to hit the slopes in Armenia's ski areas make for a beautiful winter holiday. However, be prepared for colder conditions and ensure you pack properly.

3. Packing Essentials for Different Seasons:

Packing the right basics for your trip ensures you're prepared for the various weather conditions you might experience in Armenia. Here's a more detailed plan for each season:

- Spring: Pack a mix of light and warm clothes, as the weather can change. Layers are important, as the weather can change throughout the day.

Don't forget comfortable walking shoes, a light jacket, and a hat to protect yourself from the sun.

- Summer: Lightweight and flexible clothes are important to stay comfy during warm days. Sunscreen, sunglasses, and a hat are important for defense against the strong summer sun. A reusable water bottle is handy to stay hydrated, especially if you plan on visiting outdoor places widely.

- fall: Similar to spring, clothes are important for fall. Bring along sweaters, light jackets, and comfy walking shoes. The fall colors make it a great time for shooting, so don't forget your camera.

- Winter: Winter in Armenia can be cold, especially in high-altitude places. Pack thermal clothing, jackets, a heavy coat, gloves, a scarf, and a warm hat to stay cozy. Waterproof boots or shoes are important for crossing cold or icy areas.

4. Currency and Money Matters:

Understanding the currency and money issues in Armenia is important for a hassle-free trip. The main currency is the Armenian Dram (AMD). It's smart to switch some of your home cash for Drams before your trip, as it will be useful for smaller purchases and deals.

Credit cards are widely accepted in urban areas, big hotels, and restaurants, but it's still a good idea to take some cash for more local or country places. ATMs are easily available in cities and towns, allowing you to take local cash using your foreign debit or credit card. Inform your bank about your vacation plans to ensure smooth card usage during your trip.

Keep in mind that Armenia is generally a cheap location, but it's important to spend wisely for activities, meals, and gifts. Tipping is common in restaurants, bars, and for certain services, so be familiar with the local tipping practices.

By considering these crucial aspects and making appropriate plans, you'll be all set for a unique and enriching journey to Armenia. Embrace the country's history, culture, and stunning scenery, and enjoy every moment of your adventure. Happy trips!

Chapter 3: Exploring Top Destinations

Armenia, a country rich in history, culture, and natural beauty, offers a plethora of fascinating destinations to explore. From its vibrant capital city to ancient marvels and serene national parks, every corner of Armenia promises an unforgettable experience for travelers. In this chapter, we will delve into some of the top destinations that should be on every adventurer's itinerary:

1. Yerevan: The Vibrant Capital City

As the beating heart of Armenia, Yerevan offers a captivating blend of modernity and tradition. Founded over 2,800 years ago, the city boasts a long and storied history that's evident in its architecture and culture. One of the best ways to begin your Yerevan adventure is to visit the Republic Square, a grandiose plaza adorned with elegant fountains, majestic buildings, and the famous History Museum of Armenia.

The Cascade, a massive staircase adorned with art and sculptures, is another must-visit spot, offering breathtaking panoramic views of the city and the majestic Mount Ararat in the distance.

While exploring Yerevan, don't miss the chance to immerse yourself in Armenian cuisine. The city is dotted with delightful restaurants and cafes, offering an array of delectable dishes, such as the traditional dolma, khorovats (barbecue), and lavash (thin flatbread). After indulging in the local delicacies, take a stroll along the lively streets and visit Vernissage, an open-air market where you can find everything from souvenirs and handicrafts to paintings and traditional rugs.

2. Lake Sevan: Armenia's "Blue Gem"

Known as the "Blue Gem" of Armenia, Lake Sevan is one of the largest high-altitude freshwater lakes in the world. Nestled amidst the picturesque landscapes, this pristine lake offers a tranquil escape from the bustle of city life. Surrounded by snow-capped mountains and lush greenery, Lake Sevan provides a breathtaking backdrop for a day of relaxation or exploration.

Visitors can explore the Sevanavank Monastery, perched atop the Sevan Peninsula, which offers sweeping views of the lake and the surrounding countryside. The lake's shores also offer various recreational activities such as fishing, swimming, and boat rides. For those seeking a touch of history, nearby Hayravank Monastery provides a glimpse into Armenia's religious and architectural heritage.

3. Garni and Geghard: Ancient Marvels

Delving into Armenia's ancient past, a visit to the Garni Temple and Geghard Monastery is an absolute must. Located amidst rocky cliffs and lush green valleys, Garni Temple is a well-preserved Hellenistic structure dating back to the 1st century AD. Once a pagan temple, it now stands as a testament to Armenia's rich pre-Christian history.

Just a short distance from Garni lies Geghard Monastery, an awe-inspiring complex partially carved into the surrounding cliffs. The monastery, originally known as Ayrivank, holds significant religious and cultural importance, as it is believed to have housed the spear that wounded Jesus during the crucifixion. Designated as a UNESCO World Heritage Site, Geghard Monastery's stunning architecture and spiritual atmosphere make it a profound experience for any traveler.

4. Dilijan National Park: Nature and Serenity

Escape into the lap of nature at Dilijan National Park, often referred to as "Armenia's Little Switzerland." This protected area is a paradise for nature enthusiasts, featuring dense forests, alpine meadows, and serene lakes. The park offers an array of hiking trails that lead to hidden waterfalls, ancient monasteries, and breathtaking viewpoints.

A visit to the Haghartsin Monastery within the park is a highlight. This 13th-century religious complex, surrounded by lush greenery, boasts stunning stone-carved architecture that reflects the true essence of medieval Armenian art and culture.

Chapter 4: Experiencing Armenian Culture

Armenia's rich cultural history is deeply rooted in its customs, arts, and food. In this chapter, we will dive into the heart of Armenian culture by exploring its traditional food and must-try meals, the lively world of folk music and dance events, and the fascinating arts and crafts, including Khachkars and rug-making.

1. Traditional Armenian Cuisine and Must-Try Dishes:

Armenian food is a lovely blend of tastes and culinary methods that have been passed down through generations. The food shows the country's farming history, making use of fresh and locally found products. Here are some must-try meals that will tantalize your taste buds:

- Khorovats: Armenia's version of barbecue, Khorovats features juicy chopped meat (often pork, beef, or lamb) grilled over open flames. The preserved meat is typically seasoned with traditional herbs and spices, resulting in a delicious feast.

- Dolma: Dolma is a beloved dish in Armenian cuisine, made by stuffing grape leaves with a tasty mixture of rice, chopped meat, and herbs. This dish is often served with yogurt or a garlic-based sauce for extra taste.

- Lavash: Lavash is a traditional Armenian pancake, often described as the country's "soul."

It is thin, soft, and incredibly flexible, serving as a staple in Armenian meals. UNESCO has recognized Lavash as a unique cultural property of humanity.

- Harissa: Harissa is a filling food made from slow-cooked wheat and meat (usually chicken or lamb). This traditional Armenian porridge has a warming and nutty taste, often eaten during special events and holidays.

- Armenian Barbecue: Aside from Khorovats, Armenians are passionate about barbecues, with grilled veggies and meats appearing heavily in their food. Try the different types of kebabs, seasoned with various flavorful spices.

2. Folk Music and Dance Festivals:

Armenia's folk music and dance are vital parts of its national character. The lively and passionate shows celebrate the nation's past, values, and shared experiences. Attending a folk music and dance event in Armenia is an engaging experience that gets you closer to the heart of its culture.

The "Yerevan Perspectives" International Music Festival and the "Taraz" Festival are two of the most famous music events in Armenia. These events highlight traditional Armenian music, as well as acts from different foreign singers, promoting cultural exchange and respect.

The country also hosts a range of lively dance events, where you can watch the smooth moves and colorful outfits of Armenian folk dancers. These events are not just shows but occasions for communities to come together and enjoy their history.

3. Arts and Crafts: Khachkars and Rug-Making:

Armenia boasts a rich history of arts and crafts, with some practices going back centuries. Two excellent examples of Armenian artistry are Khachkars and rug-making:

- Khachkars: Khachkars are elaborately cut cross-stones made of stone, representing the fusion of faith and art. These ornate and detailed works of art can be found in churches, graves, and different historical places throughout Armenia. Each khachkar is unique, showing the skill and creativity of Armenian artists.

- Rug-Making: Armenian rugs, known as "khlim," are made with artistic skill and hold traditional importance. The designs often show elements from nature, folklore, and holy symbols. Visiting a traditional rug-making business allows you to watch the careful process of crafting these fine pieces.

Participating in classes or exploring places dedicated to Armenian arts and crafts offers useful insights into the country's artistic history and the devotion of its artists.

Experiencing Armenian culture through its cuisine, music, dance, and arts is a fascinating journey that immerses you in the heart of this ancient and vibrant nation. Embrace the tastes, sounds, and artistic works that shape Armenia's character, and you'll carry a piece of its cultural fabric with you wherever you go.

Chapter 5: Outdoor Adventures

Armenia's beautiful scenery and diverse terrain make it an outdoor enthusiast's paradise. In this chapter, we'll explore some of the exciting outdoor adventures you can take on in Armenia, including hiking in the Armenian Highlands, skiing in Tsaghkadzor and Jermuk, and exploring diving and spelunking possibilities.

1. Hiking in the Armenian Highlands:

The Armenian Highlands offers a wealth of hiking trails that cater to both beginner walkers and expert hikers wanting a challenge. The high-altitude plateaus, green rivers, and grand mountains provide beautiful settings for your outdoor activities.

One of the most famous hiking sites is the Dilijan National Park, offering a network of well-marked trails that lead you through thick woods, beautiful fields, and crystal-clear streams. The Transcaucasian Trail, still under development, will eventually cross Armenia, offering a unique chance for long-distance walkers to discover the country's varied scenery.

For the more daring, try going to the top of Mount Aragats, the highest hill in Armenia. The rise offers panoramic views of the nearby farmland, making it a satisfying experience for nature lovers and thrill-seekers alike.

2. Skiing in Tsaghkadzor and Jermuk:

Armenia's winter beauty calls ski and snowboard fans to hit the slopes in Tsaghkadzor and Jermuk. These two mountain towns offer excellent services and fresh snow during the winter season, drawing locals and foreign tourists alike.

Tsaghkadzor, located just an hour's drive from Yerevan, is a famous ski area known for its well-groomed slopes and modern services. Whether you're a newbie or an experienced skier, Tsaghkadzor has something to offer everyone. The lodge also offers other winter sports such as snow sledding and hiking.

Jermuk, on the other hand, is more than just a ski stop; it is also known for its hot mineral springs, making it an ideal spot for après-ski relaxing. The resort's natural beauty, with snow-capped mountains surrounding the area, adds to the charm of the winter experience.

3. Caving and Spelunking Opportunities:

Armenia's natural scenery boasts an amazing number of caves, giving spelunking and diving chances for adventure lovers. These underground wonders are rich in rock formations and often hold cultural and historical importance.

The Areni-1 Cave, located in the Vayots Dzor Province, is an archeological place where the world's oldest known winery was found. Exploring this cave allows you to step back in time and watch the early roots of wine production.

The Mozrov Cave, located in the Syunik Province, is another famous diving location. This complicated cave system has vast rooms and tight pathways, providing an exciting and difficult experience for spelunkers.

As caving and spelunking activities require specialized tools and knowledge, it's recommended to join planned tours led by experienced guides who can ensure your safety and improve your understanding of the caves' geological and historical importance.

From the peaks of the Armenian Highlands to the slopes of Tsaghkadzor and Jermuk and the secret depths of Armenia's caves, the country offers a wide range of outdoor activities for thrill-seekers and nature lovers.

Embrace the stunning scenery and lose yourself in the natural beauty of Armenia as you embark on unforgettable outdoor experiences. Always value safety and respect the environment to ensure the protection of these pure places for future generations of explorers.

Chapter 6: Understanding Armenian History

Armenia's past is deeply linked with its cultural and religious traditions. In this chapter, we will look into some of the key historical places that hold significant importance in Armenian history, including the Etchmiadzin Cathedral, the Armenian Genocide Memorial Complex, and the Khor Virap Monastery.

1. Etchmiadzin Cathedral: The Spiritual Center of Armenia

The Etchmiadzin Cathedral, situated in the town of Vagharshapat, is one of the most holy sites in Armenia and the center of the Armenian Apostolic Church. It holds great religious and historical importance, as it is thought to be the oldest church in the world.

Constructed in the early 4th century AD, the church was built upon the orders of Saint Gregory the Illuminator, who played a key role in turning Armenia to Christianity, making it the first country to accept Christianity as its state faith in 301 AD. The cathedral's building style displays a unique mix of Armenian, Roman, and Byzantine elements.

The cathedral's interior is decorated with beautiful religious artwork, old relics, and religious objects, including the Holy Lance, said to be the spear that pierced Jesus during the execution. Etchmiadzin continues to be a major travel place for Armenians and Christians worldwide, drawing followers wanting spiritual comfort and historical knowledge.

2. Armenian Genocide Memorial Complex:

The Armenian Genocide Monument Complex, also known as Tsitsernakaberd, is a serious and deeply moving monument dedicated to the victims of the Armenian Genocide. The memorial is situated on a hill facing Yerevan, the capital city, and consists of several elements that represent the sad events of the past.

The center feature of the complex is the Memorial light, an endless light that burns in memory of the 1.5 million Armenians who lost their lives during the massacre committed by the Ottoman Empire from 1915 to 1923. Surrounding the flame are twelve basalt rocks, representing the twelve lost areas of ancient Armenia.

The museum within the complex offers a complete historical account of the killing, showing objects, photos, and personal testimonials to honor the memory of the victims and protect their legacy for future generations.

Visiting the Armenian Genocide Memorial Complex is a sad yet important experience, as it offers tourists an opportunity to think about one of the darkest chapters in Armenian history while giving respect to the perseverance and strength of the Armenian people.

3. Khor Virap Monastery: A Historic Pilgrimage Site:

The Khor Virap Monastery, located near the Turkish border, is a famous feature and a treasured religious spot in Armenia. Its past is closely linked to Saint Gregory the Illuminator, who was imprisoned here by King Tiridates III for 13 years due to his Christian faith.

According to tradition, it was Saint Gregory's prayers that led to the miracle healing of King Tiridates III from a serious illness. As a result, the king turned to Christianity, marking the beginning of Armenia's conversion to the new faith.

The monastery's position offers stunning views of Mount Ararat, the holy sign of Armenia and an important part of the country's cultural character. The calm atmosphere and historical importance make Khor Virap an important stop for tourists looking to connect with Armenia's spiritual heritage and study its old history.

Understanding Armenian history is a meaningful and educational trip, deeply linked with its spiritual, cultural, and political experiences. These historical places represent important parts of Armenia's story, acting as memories of the country's resilience, faith, and the importance of saving its history for future generations.

Chapter 7: Practical Tips for Travelers

Traveling to Armenia can be a satisfying and educational experience. To ensure an easy and enjoyable trip, it's important to prepare yourself with useful tips for tourists. In this chapter, we'll cover language and conversation tips, local practices and etiquette, transportation options within Armenia, and health and medical concerns.

1. Language and Communication Tips:

- Language: Armenian is the national language of Armenia. While many Armenians speak some level of English, especially in urban areas and famous tourist spots, it's always helpful to learn a few basic Armenian words to improve your contacts with locals. Simple greetings like "Barev" (hello) and "Shnorhakal em" (thank you) go a long way in making a good impression.

- Cyrillic Script: In Armenia, the Armenian alphabet is used, and it is written in the unique Armenian script. Although road signs and public information often have readings in both Armenian and English, it can be helpful to familiarize yourself with Cyrillic writing to move through the country more effectively.

- Language Apps: Consider getting language apps or phrasebooks to help you with translations and conversation during your trip.

2. Local Customs and Etiquette:

- Respect Religious Sites: Armenia is deeply rooted in religious customs, and many sites hold spiritual importance. When visiting churches, temples, and other holy places, dress modestly, and avoid taking photos in forbidden areas.

- Greetings: Armenians are known for their warm welcome. When meeting new people, offer a friendly welcome with a handshake, and keep eye contact while talking.

- Tipping: Tipping is common in restaurants, bars, and for certain services. It is usually welcomed to leave a tip of around 10% of the bill for good service.

- Gift Giving: If asked to someone's home, bringing a small gift, such as candies or flowers, is a nice offering.

3. Transportation Options within Armenia:

- Public Transport: Armenia has a well-developed public transportation system, including buses and minibusses known as "marshrutkas." These choices are cheap and connect major cities and towns. However, remember that the plans may not always be accurate.

- Taxis: Taxis are easily available in cities and towns. It's recommended to discuss the price before starting the trip or use paid cabs.

- Renting a Car: Renting a car is a handy choice for visiting the country's more rural places at your own pace. Make sure to have a foreign driving pass and prepare yourself with local driving rules.

- Yerevan Metro: The Yerevan Metro is a quick and efficient way to get around the main city. It consists of two lines and links major sites and neighborhoods.

4. Health and Medical Considerations:

- Medical Insurance: Before going to Armenia, ensure that you have comprehensive medical insurance that covers any unforeseen health problems.

- Medications: If you are on prescription medications, bring an adequate amount for your trip and carry them in their original labeled cases.

- Drinking Water: While tap water is usually safe in Yerevan and other big towns, it's suggested to drink bottled water in rural areas to avoid any possible stomach problems.

- Altitude Considerations: If you plan on going or flying to high-altitude places, be aware of the possible effects of altitude sickness. Take it easy during your first few days at higher levels and stay well-hydrated.

- Travel vaccines: Consult your healthcare provider or a travel medicine expert to ask about advised vaccines for travel to Armenia.

By keeping these useful tips in mind, you can improve your travel experience in Armenia, ensuring a more engaging and culturally sensitive trip. Embrace the country's rich past, warm kindness, and beautiful scenery as you explore all that Armenia has to offer

Chapter 8: Staying Connected and Safe

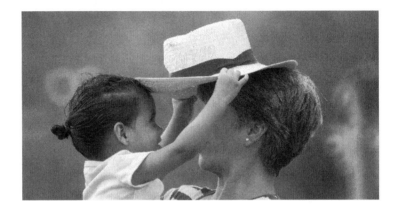

As a tourist in Armenia, staying connected and ensuring your safety are important objectives. In this chapter, we'll cover various aspects of staying connected, including internet and cell connection, as well as important emergency contacts and services.

Additionally, we'll provide you with useful tips for keeping safe during your trip.

1. Internet and Mobile Connectivity:

- Internet Access: Internet access is widely available in Armenia, especially in urban areas and big tourist locations. Many hotels, bars, and restaurants give free Wi-Fi to their customers. Additionally, you can find internet shops in cities and towns, offering cheap internet access.

- Local SIM Card: To stay online while on the go, consider buying a local SIM card. You can find SIM cards from big cell network companies like VivaCell-MTS, Beeline, and Ucom. They offer different data and call deals that are fairly priced.

- Roaming: If you wish to use your foreign SIM card, check with your cell company about roaming choices and costs. Keep in mind that foreign transfer rates can be expensive, so it's best to use local SIM cards for more cheap choices.

2. Emergency Contacts and Services:

- Emergency Number: The international emergency number in Armenia is 911. This number can be called for police, fire, and emergencies.

- Tourist Support: Armenia offers tourist support centers in big towns like Yerevan, where visitors can seek help and information. The Tourist Support Centers are prepared to provide advice in multiple languages and can help with any travel-related questions.

3. Tips for Staying Safe During Your Trip:

- Be Vigilant in busy Places: Like in any other place, be careful of your things, especially in busy areas and tourist sites. Keep your belongings safe and avoid showing expensive things.

- Respect Local Customs: Familiarize yourself with local customs and practices to avoid any unintentional harm. Dress modestly when viewing holy places and follow any rules or directions given.

- Use Licensed Transportation: When using cars or other transportation services, opt for licensed providers to ensure your safety and avoid possible scams.

- Stay in Well-Lit Areas: When visiting towns at night, stick to well-lit and busy areas. Avoid badly lit or remote places, especially if you're going alone.

- Follow Government warnings: Check for any travel warnings released by your government for Armenia before and during your trip. Stay updated about any safety or security issues that may impact your trip plans.

- Keep Important Documents Safe: Make photocopies of your passport, visa, trip insurance, and other important documents. Keep the copies separate from the originals, and consider keeping digital copies in a safe cloud storage account.

- Travel Insurance: Ensure you have complete travel insurance that covers medical situations, trip delays, and other unforeseen events.

- Be Cautious with booze: If you choose to drink booze, do so wisely. Overindulgence can weaken judgment and make you open to crashes or incidents.

By staying aware and taking proper steps, you can enjoy a safe and enjoyable trip to Armenia. Embrace the country's culture, discover its historical wonders, and immerse yourself in the natural beauty while keeping your safety a top concern.

Chapter 9: Responsible Travel and Sustainability

As tourists, it's important to be aware of our effect on the earth and local communities. In this part, we will study environment-friendly practices in Armenia and ways to support local communities and companies to ensure responsible travel and survival.

1. Environment-Friendly Practices in Armenia:

- Respect for Nature: Armenia is blessed with beautiful scenery, different ecosystems, and unique wildlife. As responsible tourists, we should value nature by following marked paths, not upsetting wildlife, and avoiding dumping or leaving behind any waste.

- Sustainable Transportation: Opt for eco-friendly transportation choices whenever possible. Consider using public transport, walking, or riding to discover cities and towns. If renting a car, choose fuel-efficient or hybrid cars.

- Reduce Plastic Use: Armenia, like many countries, faces difficulties with plastic trash. Minimize your use of single-use plastics by bringing a reusable water bottle, shopping bag, and tools.

- Water Conservation: Armenia suffers rare water shortages, especially during the dry season. Conserve water by taking shorter baths, turning off taps when not in use, and reusing towels in accommodations.

- Responsible Camping: If you plan on camping, choose approved camping places and leave no record of your visit. Dispose of trash properly and avoid hurting plants.

- Support Environmental projects: Consider backing local groups and projects that work towards environmental protection and survival in Armenia. Volunteer options with these groups may also be possible.

2. Supporting Local Communities and Businesses:

- Stay in Locally-Owned Accommodations: Choose hotels, guesthouses, or homestays that are locally owned and run. This helps to directly add to the local economy and support the lives of local people.

- Shop Local: Purchase gifts, crafts, and goods from local artists and shops. This helps protect traditional crafts and supports local communities economically.

- Dine at Local Restaurants: Try traditional Armenian fare at locally-owned restaurants, cafes, and street food stalls. Embracing local tastes not only helps local businesses but also promotes cultural exchange.

- Engage with Local Culture: Take part in cultural activities, fairs, and events planned by local groups. This develops mutual understanding and respect between tourists and locals.

- Responsible Tourism companies: When participating in activities such as camping, wildlife tours, or adventure sports, choose tour companies that value responsible and sustainable practices.

- accept Local Customs: Learn about and accept the local customs, habits, and social norms of the places you visit. This shows ethnic awareness and respect for their way of life.

- Leave Positive Footprints: Make a positive effect during your visit by working on community projects or joining in clean-up efforts. Consider giving a gift to help with neighborhood development activities.

Example: One way to help local communities in Armenia is by visiting the Armenian town of Lernagog. This town is part of a community-based tourism project, where local families offer housing and lodging and host tourists for cultural experiences.

Travelers can join in farming activities, watch traditional Armenian music and dance shows, and learn about the village's cultural history. By choosing to stay in Lernagog and participating in these activities, tourists directly support the local economy and help keep the traditional way of life in the town.

By practicing responsible travel and helping local communities, you can contribute to the protection of Armenia's cultural and natural history while having a good effect on the places you visit.

Responsible tourism ensures that future generations can continue to enjoy the beauty and uniqueness of Armenia while promoting sustainable growth for the country.

Chapter 10: Useful Phrases in Armenian

As a tourist in Armenia, learning a few simple words in Armenian can go a long way in making your contacts with locals more fun and beneficial.

While many Armenians speak some level of English, using a few words in the local language shows respect and love for the country's culture. Here are some important words and terms for travelers:

1. Basic Greetings:

- Hello: Բարև (Barev)
- Goodbye: Յտեսություն (Tstesutyun)
- Please: խնդրում եմ (Khndrum yem)
- Thank you: Շնորհակալ եմ (Shnorhakal em)
- You're welcome: Կարիք չունես (Karik chunes)
- Excuse me / Sorry: Ներում եմ (Nerum em)

2. Basic Conversational Phrases:

- Yes: Այո (Ayo)
- No: Ոչ (Voch)
- How are you?: Ողջույն, ինչպես եք (Voghjuyn, inchpes ek?)
- I'm fine, thank you: Լավն եմ, շնորհակալ եմ (Lavn em, shnorhakal em)
- What is your name?: Ի՞նչ է ձեր անունը (Inch e dzer anuny?)
- My name is [Your Name]: Իմ անունն է [Your Name] (Im anunn e [Your Name])

3. Numbers:

- One: մեկ (mek)
- Two: երկու (yerek'u)
- Three: երեք (yerek')
- Four: չորս (chors)
- Five: հինգ (hing)
- Ten: տասներկու (tasnerku)

4. Asking for Help:

- I need help: Oգնություն պետք ունեմ (Ognut'yun petk unem)
- Where is [place]?: [place]-ը ուր է (place-u ur e?)
- I'm lost: Կորցրել եմ (Korts'rel em)

5. Ordering Food:

- I would like [dish]: Ես ուզում եմ [dish] (Yes uzum em [dish])
- Water: Ջուր (Joor)
- Beer: Բիրա (Bira)
- Wine: Գինի (Gini)

6. Getting Around:

- Where is the bus stop?: Որոգուտ կայքի կողմից ու՞ր է (Vorogut kayki koghmits uur e)
- How much is the ticket?: Որքան է գումարը (Vorqan e gumary)

7. Expressing Gratitude:

- Thank you very much: Շնորհակալ եմ շատ (Shnorhakal em shat)
- You are very kind: Դուք շատ բարի եք (Dook shat bari ek)

Remember, even trying to use a few words in Armenian will be welcomed by the locals and can help break the ice in your conversations. Armenians are known for their warm welcome, and showing respect for their language and culture will only improve your trip experience in this beautiful country.

Made in the USA
Coppell, TX
05 June 2024